JAPAN, THE AMBIGUOUS, AND MYSELF

JAPAN,
THE AMBIGUOUS,
AND MYSELF

The Nobel Prize Speech
and Other Lectures

Kenzaburo Oe

KODANSHA INTERNATIONAL
Tokyo New York London

EDITOR'S NOTE
With the approval of the author, some stylistic revisions have been made to the original English texts of these lectures.

ACKNOWLEDGMENT
The second and third lectures in this collection were given under the auspices, respectively, of The Wheatland Foundation and the Center for International Studies at Duke University. "Japan's Dual Identity" was first published in *Postmodernism and Japan*, edited by M. Miyoshi and H. D. Harootunian (Duke University Press, 1989).

Distributed in the United States by Kodansha America, Inc., 114 Fifth Avenue, New York, N.Y. 10011, and in the United Kingdom and continental Europe by Kodansha Europe Ltd., 95 Aldwych, London WC2B 4JF. Published by Kodansha International Ltd., 17-14 Otowa 1-chome, Bunkyo-ku, Tokyo 112, and Kodansha America, Inc. Nobel Prize lecture copyright © 1994 by The Nobel Foundation. Other lectures © 1992, 1990, 1986 by Kenzaburo Oe. All rights reserved. Printed in Japan.
First edition, 1995
ISBN 4-7700-1980-7
95 96 97 98 99 10 9 8 7 6 5 4 3 2 1

CONTENTS

Speaking on Japanese Culture before a Scandinavian Audience

Lecture series, 1992

Translated by Kunioki Yanagishita

I

I have always been strongly attracted to the countries of Scandinavia, though this is my first visit. Coming here, in fact, has been a dream of mine ever since I was a child; yet this very dream, in some strange way, has prevented me from coming sooner.

As some of you may know, I grew up during the war in a small village deep in the heavily forested valleys of the island of Shikoku. In those days it was virtually impossible for me to lay my hands on books or magazines that might tell me something about foreign lands. Nevertheless, I did have the good fortune to find one such book, intriguingly entitled *The Wonderful Adventures of Nils*, which I read with a child's intense excitement. I remember, too, that this book was somehow lost, and by the time I was in high school I had come to doubt it had ever existed, wondering if it had been nothing more than a childhood vision—a feeling that was tied to my growing belief in the impossibility of there being any such thing as "perfect fiction." You can imagine my surprise, then, when I came across the book again during my university days. I learned then that what I had read was not a translation but a retelling in Japanese of a story by a writer named Lagerlöf.

I remember how entranced I was as a child with each of Nils's adventures, but I also remember thinking that the hero had an odd and slightly disturbing personality. The story tells of his becoming a dwarf and riding away on a wild goose to join its flock; and only after a fierce battle in which Nils risks his life to save one of the geese is he able to rid himself of his warped character, undergoing a complete transformation. I believe that even as a child I somehow understood this story as an allegory of human life. Furthermore, though I could never have explained this to my parents or friends—or even to myself, perhaps—

I sensed, even then, a certain sensuality, an erotic passion, if you will, in Nils's relationship with the goose. I imagined some sort of union between tiny Nils and the overpowering, yet kindly, female goose. In any event, this story left an indelible impression on me, like a childhood scar still visible on a grown man; and it was also my first encounter with Scandinavia, one that I still associate with a longing for travel and faraway places.

A wanderlust similar to Nils's is present in the works of Karen Blixen, a Danish writer I like very much. Blixen, though suffering from a venereal disease which in her day was often fatal, left her native land to go to Africa, where she started a coffee plantation and wrote her much-admired letters. With the onset of the Second World War, however, she was forced to return to Denmark, where she cooperated with the resistance and longed for the Africa she had lost. And toward the end of the war, to continue this chain of associations, it was to this same Denmark that the French writer Louis-Ferdinand Céline fled from a remote village in Germany, escaping across a ruined and burning continent. Céline had been labeled a Nazi sympathizer, and was therefore unable to return to France. Now Céline has always struck me as an adult version of the wicked Nils, so it was perhaps appropriate that while making his escape he encountered a group of mentally retarded children on a train and decided, much as Nils did, to risk his life to help them reach Sweden. This act of random kindness is, for me, evidence of what I would like to call Céline's innocent longing for Scandinavia. I have written about him in my novel *Shizukana seikatsu*.

In another work of mine, *Women Who Listen to the Rain Tree*, I wrote about the English novelist Malcolm Lowry who, like Blixen and Céline, lived much of his life away from his home country. Lowry became, in a sense, the hidden protagonist of my novel. His manner of living was, I feel, deeply related to his writing, a fact apparent in *Under the Volcano*, a novel that vividly portrays the life of a foreigner in Mexico. Lowry, as is well known, was an alcoholic, and the accident that brought about his untimely death was quite likely caused by his drinking. In the end, his life was one of continual suffering which left him broken and unbalanced, yet together with this sadness was a certain carefree innocence, which can be observed in something as insignificant as his love of the ukelele. It is perhaps a symptom of the Nils syndrome I suffer from that I am so fascinated by people like this. At any rate, Lowry too must have been affected by the same wanderlust at an early age since he took a leave of absence from his university and shipped out as a sailor on an ocean liner; and it was this experience, a marriage of his longing for both the sea and distant lands, that became the basis for his first efforts as a writer, encouraged, I believe, by yet another Scandinavian, the Norwegian writer Nordahl Grieg, who I understand was distantly related to Edvard Grieg, the composer.

Having always wanted to write about the sea and about life at sea, Lowry, while barely twenty years old, had found the perfect model for the kind of work he wished to produce in a translation of one of Grieg's novels. He was so excited that he wrote several letters to Grieg, who was then living in Oslo, but, perhaps typically of Lowry—and what I like so much about him—

he never summoned up the courage to post them. Instead, he went to Norway himself and, after a certain amount of searching, was at last able to meet his hero. This encounter came about, I believe, because Lowry, like others of us, had always looked wistfully toward Scandinavia, and the affection I feel for him is not unrelated to this shared taste for the countries of Northern Europe.

In yet another novel of mine, *Jinsei no shinseki*, I wrote about two young brothers, one of whom is handicapped, who choose to take their own lives. The work concerns their mother's grief and her search for a way to atone for their deaths. I was surprised to learn that this novel has been re-told quite beautifully as a children's story by the Swedish writer Emilia Lindgren, and I am very grateful to her.

I owe much as well to the work of the psychologist Erik Eriksen whose theory of identity stresses the importance of finding one's true place in life. As someone who left his native village and has lived his life away from it, I could empathize with Eriksen from my first encounter with his writing, and particularly with the shadow that seems to hang over his soul at the loss of his Scandinavian home. And it is now nearly half a century since the shadow of Nils's high-flying goose swept over me, leaving its mark and helping to determine the shape my life would take. It has been a shadow in the sense that it provides no concrete "reality" from which I can seek guidance; rather, like an invisible magnetic field, it pulls me toward something remote, unseen, the longing for which has become a lifelong habit. But a romantic word like "longing" is perhaps misleading in describing the force it has, and it may have been my awareness of this underlying and slightly unnerving power that kept me from coming to Scandinavia sooner.

From Swedenborg's mysticism to Bergman's films, I have been attracted by many things Scandinavian, lending an always attentive ear to each call I heard from this quarter. And I would only add that the music of Scandinavia has all along served to reinforce my understanding of the many Scandinavians who have touched my heart.

II

I want to talk today about Japanese culture as seen
through the filter of literature, and to do so I will
focus on three main subjects, the first of which
is *The Tale of Genji*. This tenth-century "novel,"
considered the pride and joy of Japanese culture,
appeared three hundred years before Dante's
Divine Comedy. Some fifty-four chapters in length,
it was written by Murasaki Shikibu, a lady-in-
waiting at the imperial court. The theme of particular interest to me in this work is introduced in
the chapter entitled "The Maiden," in which
Genji, the hero, now in his mid-thirties, has risen
to the post of first minister, the highest position in
court politics, second only to the emperor himself.
The chapter deals with the youthful love affairs
and education of Genji's son, Yugiri, and I would
like to comment specifically on the latter: his son's
education.

Yugiri is to attend university, or, to be more
exact, enter the university dormitory at court
where young boys his age are matriculated. But
when Genji sends him to the dormitory, Yugiri's

grandmother, an imperial princess, objects strenuously to the idea of a child of noble birth being forced into the kind of studies usually left to striving commoners. "This," she laments, "is the very height of absurdity. How pitiful!" And the narrator seconds the grandmother's objection, agreeing that Genji's proposal is inappropriate. Yet Murasaki Shikibu has Genji reason with the old princess, arguing in favor of the importance of learning and saying that he himself had benefited from even the inadequate knowledge he was able to acquire in the service of his father, the emperor. "Only after we have had enough book learning," Genji explains, "can we bring our Yamato spirit into full play"—Yamato being an old name for Japan. By "book learning" Genji means knowledge of Chinese literature; so he is arguing that it is only after establishing a solid foundation in the Chinese classics that intrinsically Japanese talents will be treated with due respect.

"Yamato spirit." Those of you who have studied modern history may hear an ominous echo in this expression, for it came to take on a dangerous overtone in the earlier half of this century as the battle cry of Japanese soldiers pressing forward on their march of aggression into China. But I would like to note here that the words first appeared in *The Tale of Genji*, coined by a woman writer with the specific and limited meaning I have just described. I believe she had in mind something not unlike what Aristotle calls *sensus communis*, that is, a shared sensibility. And if we further define this *sensus communis* as an innate quality that exists in human beings at a higher level comprising our intellect, emotions, and imagination, we could say that when Murasaki Shikibu speaks of "Yamato spirit," she is referring to nothing more than a particular sensibility inherent in her fellow countrymen. "Having Yamato spirit is important," she has Genji say, and he goes on to argue that this "shared sensibility" should influence one's behavior as a human being. But without a solid foundation in Chinese learning, its benefits are limited, and so, he concludes, his son should study at the university.

Such formal education has, in fact, been the means by which the Japanese have, from ancient times, sought to learn about foreign cultures. Traditionally, that meant Chinese culture, which the

Japanese in the past studied with a certain confidence in their own "shared sensibility." Nor, I think, was this confidence a sign of hubris or intolerance; rather, it was marked by the kind of gentle sensitivity characteristic of human beings who know what it means to doubt. Such was Genji's confidence, born of a clear-eyed practicality and realism—and contrasted here with the class-bound notions of the old princess.

After the Meiji Restoration of 1868, "foreign culture" came to mean not Chinese but European learning, with all the implications that had for the modernization of Japan; but fundamentally there was no real change in the attitude toward learning from those outside. Once again, however, the notion of "Yamato spirit" was brought into play, as Meiji politicians used it to unify the people's cultural consciousness in the interests of creating a modern state. This was done, in large part, by stressing the absolute nature of Japanese culture, with the emperor as its central feature. From there, however, it was only a short step for the concept of "Yamato spirit" to assume its role as a slogan for imperialist Japan.

In the same period, the similar expression *wakon-kansai*, or "Yamato spirit with Chinese learning," was replaced by *wakon-yosai*, "Yamato spirit with Western learning"; and this, too, gradually took on a belligerent, militaristic connotation. No one would have denied that we learned extensively from Western science, art, and technology, yet Japan's ideology, which held the emperor to be absolute, was always placed above all that. This sort of absolutism, which showed none of the tolerance and sensitivity that characterized the spirit to which Genji was referring, led eventually to the fanatic belief that Japan could win a war despite trailing far behind in modern weapons technology and other similar areas. I know firsthand about such fanaticism, since it was instilled in me as a child. Like everyone else at that time, I was made to believe this mad conviction so alien to the "Yamato spirit" of Murasaki Shikibu. She put it very well when she said that "without *learning* it serves no purpose."

III

Japan's greatest writer after the Meiji Restoration is Soseki Natsume, who lived during a period of rapid modernization, and it is his work I would like to take up next.

Among his best-known works is a novel entitled *Sorekara* or, in English, *And Then*. Written in 1909, in the relatively peaceful years following the Russo-Japanese War, it portrays the life of Daisuke, a young, well-to-do intellectual who falls in love with the wife of a friend and finds himself entangled in all the torments this entails. The novel is of particular interest to me because the hero is in the habit of bluntly expressing his criticism of the society he lived in. At one point, for example, when a friend asks him why he refuses to work and remains dependent on his wealthy father, he unleashes the following tirade. (I quote here from Norma Field's translation.)

> "Why not?—well, it's not my fault.
> That's to say, it's the world's fault. Or,
> to exaggerate a little, it's because the

relationship between Japan and the West is no good that I won't work.... The point is, Japan can't get along without borrowing from the West.... But it poses as a first-class power. And it's straining to join the ranks of the first-class powers. That's why, in every direction, it puts up the façade of a first-class power and cheats on what's behind.... And see, the consequences are reflected in each of us as individuals. A people so oppressed by the West have no mental leisure, they can't do anything worthwhile. They get an education that's stripped to the bare bones, and they're driven with their noses to the grindstone until they're dizzy—that's why they all end up with nervous breakdowns.... Unfortunately, exhaustion of the spirit and deterioration of the body come hand-in-hand. And that's not all. The decline of morality has set in too. Look where you will in this country,

you won't find one square inch of
brightness. It's all pitch black. So what
difference would it make, what I said
or what I did, me standing all alone in
the middle of it?"

This is, of course, Soseki himself speaking his mind,
as is the following. (Again I quote from Field's
translation.)

Contemporary society, in which no
human being could have contact with
another without feeling contemptu-
ous, constituted what Daisuke called
the decadence of the twentieth century. The life appetites, which had
suddenly swollen of late, exerted
extreme pressure on the instinct for
morality and threatened its collapse.
Daisuke regarded this phenomenon
as a clash between the old and new
appetites. And finally, he understood
that the striking growth of the life
appetites was, in effect, a tidal wave
that had swept from European shores.

The two forces would have to come to an equilibrium at some point. But Daisuke believed that until the day came when feeble Japan could stand shoulder to shoulder financially with the greatest powers of Europe, that balance would not be achieved. And he was resigned to the likelihood that the sun would never shine upon such a day.

Elsewhere in the novel Soseki refers to the Japanese as "an unfortunate people beset by the fierce appetites of life," and he laments that European morality is unknown to them. I would only add that this description applies equally well to the Japanese today. The "fierce appetites" of the Japanese in the 1990s, manifested in every aspect of our greedy consumerism, all but dwarf those of Soseki's time and continue to be driven by what he calls "tidal waves that sweep from European shores." Status-conferring brand-name products from Europe fill the shelves of Japanese stores from Tokyo to the smallest provincial town, and the anonymous mass of Japanese consumers line up to buy them, eager to satisfy this strange craving of theirs. The young are especially ravenous in this regard, but corporate moguls are not far behind, as they have shown recently with such conspicuous purchases as Rockefeller Center and van Gogh's *Sunflowers*. One might imagine that these world-class shopping sprees would come under attack from the Japanese public, but they haven't, in large part because people realize that the corporate giants are only doing on a grander scale what each of them is doing privately. People who live in glass houses, as we all know, do not throw stones.

Soseki's gloomy judgments were prophetic in every way but one: he could never have known that the day would come when Japan would be able to "stand shoulder to shoulder financially with the greatest powers of Europe." That day *has* come, but without the beneficial effect that Soseki imagined it would have: the balance between "appetites" and morality has not been restored, and the spiritual deficit has become more acute. True, Japan has been modernized, but at the cost of an ugly war which it started in China and which left neighboring Asian countries devastated. Japan itself was reduced to a smoldering ruin; Tokyo was razed to the ground, and a worse fate befell Hiroshima and Nagasaki. Still, modernization continued with the postwar reconstruction and the subsequent period of rapid economic growth; but these have, in effect, led to a deeper kind of decline, a state of outright spiritual poverty. In this sense, Soseki was correct, frighteningly correct.

Soseki's astute predictions present us, however, not only with a bleak vision but with a task to fulfill, one that has to do with what he called an "appetite for morality." From *Sorekara*, it is clear that Japanese intellectuals of Soseki's time possessed a European sense of morality, which they were able to connect with that held by the Japanese before the beginning of their march toward modernization. If Japan is to find a way out of its current predicament—-by which I mean its lack of any moral direction—then it must do so by establishing a sense of morality that can be shared with Western nations but that, for its own purposes, is founded firmly on the traditions of Japan's premodern period. Only then will Japan be able to shed its "black sheep" image and play an appropriate role in the world community.

The world is changing, and not just in Eastern Europe. Values are becoming ever more diverse, and with this diversification come new goals and aspirations. In this changed world, Japan will inevitably have a new part to play, perhaps not the least important aspect of which will be in its relationship with a changing China.

IV

The third writer I would like to talk about is myself, though I should hasten to add that I am not suggesting that I belong in the same league as Murasaki or Soseki. Still, if you will indulge me, I would like to spend a few minutes on two of my works that have been translated into several European languages.

A Personal Matter is the story of a young man whose first child is born with a cranial deformity.

The work describes what might be called a rite of passage, as the young father struggles to accept the infant as a member of his family. When he first sees the baby lying in the hospital crib, he hopes it will die, thinking that in life it would be just a vegetable and fearing the burden that he and his wife would face for the rest of their lives. In the course of the story, the young man in fact does more than merely wish for the baby's death; he desperately searches the city for a doctor who will agree to let the child die.

The young man I describe is, in a sense, a romantic. Before marrying, he had dreamed of going to Africa, and it is this dream that comes back to him with a vengeance when faced with the reality of having become the father of a deformed child. Having the child killed, divorcing his wife, and fleeing Japan—these are the nightmare fantasies that occur to him, prompted in part by a former girlfriend who does everything she can to make them come true. In the end, however, the young man experiences a kind of epiphany, realizing that abandoning the child to die is tantamount to destroying himself. He sheds his romanticism, parts with the girlfriend who is bound for Africa, and accepts the child, deciding in favor of a life-saving operation. His decision is for reality: to build a family on reality, to live reality.

The novel *Man'en gannen no futtoboru*, translated into English as *The Silent Cry*, is structurally more complex than *A Personal Matter*. It has to do with two very symbolic years in Japanese history: 1860 and 1960. In 1860, just before embarking on its program of modernization, the feudal government sent delegates to America for the first time; and in 1960, exactly one hundred years later, the security treaty with America, negotiated at the end of the Pacific War, was extended. In that year, a popular movement demanding the treaty's nullification swept the nation, but the will of the people who took part in anti-treaty demonstrations was ignored. One of the heroes of *The Silent Cry* is a college student named Takashi who takes part in these demonstrations. After the defeat of the movement, he has a change of heart, converting to the pro-treaty side and going to America as a member of a theatrical troupe to give performances expressing his remorse to the American public. Returning to Japan, he decides to leave Tokyo, the scene of his political activities, and go back to the land of his ancestors, a village in a valley in Shikoku surrounded by forests. And he invites his elder brother, Mitsusaburo, to make the journey with him, though neither has visited the village in a long time. Mitsusaburo, who was no more than a disinterested observer of the anti-treaty movement, reluctantly agrees to join him.

Soon after their arrival in the village, the brothers, while searching an old storehouse attached to their family residence, discover records telling of events that had taken place a hundred years earlier. Their great-grandfather had been a village official who had crushed a peasant rebellion led by his own younger brother. They learn, too, from village legend, that their great-grandfather had lured his brother to the very same storehouse and had murdered him there. As the story unfolds, Takashi, on the pretext of organizing a football team, gathers a group of young men together and trains them to attack a new supermarket that has been built with Korean money. The attack throws the village into a state of anarchy, and the two brothers, almost despite themselves, begin to take on the roles played by their counterparts a hundred years earlier. Before the drama can fully play itself out, however, Takashi's rebellion, which he calls "a riot of the imagination," runs aground on his involvement in a sex crime perpetrated in the guise of an accident. Cornered, he commits suicide, but his death awakens Mitsusaburo to a life of action.

One of the motives I had for writing this novel was my growing awareness at the time of a culture in Japan that was very different from the dominant Tokyo one. The work is set in my native village in Shikoku, but even that village is a part of Japan that was undergoing a major transition then. After the defeat in the Pacific War, reconstruction according to a mandate issued by Tokyo was carried out in every corner of the country, my village being no exception. This was, in fact, part of the reason I had to leave to study at a university in Tokyo, though this has been the pattern for nearly every intellectual in Japan in recent times, and I was merely following a well-trodden path. In my case, I majored in French literature and began my career as a writer. I remained in Tokyo after graduating, and, like Takashi in the novel, I was involved in the 1960 movement against the U.S.-Japan Security Treaty. But for me, at the time, this experience led not so much back to my village but to a growing awareness of and interest in Okinawa, a prefecture that was then still under U.S. occupation. In particular, it was the cultural independence of this island prefecture that planted in me a seed that has grown into a new perspective on Japanese culture as a whole. For no matter how Japanized (or "Yamatoized") it may outwardly appear now, Okinawa still retains its non-Yamato cultural identity; and, unlike the insular, unaccommodating, and emperor-focused culture of the rest of Japan, it is blessed with a richness and diversity peculiar to peripheral cultures. Its people possess an openness to the world that comes from knowing the meaning of relative values.

What I did in *The Silent Cry*, with the understanding I gained from Okinawan culture, was to identify elements in the legends of my own village that reach out to similar legends from Korea and other Asian nations. In a sense, the novel becomes what Mikhail Bakhtin calls, in the phraseology of European culture, "an image system of grotesque realism"; and it was, in fact, Bakhtin's theory that enabled me to make these cultural connections. In the process of doing so, moreover, I was able to rediscover and represent aspects of Okinawa that are embedded deep within other peripheral Japanese cultures.

The surname or, more accurately perhaps, the clan name of the brothers in the novel is Nedokoro, which means "the place of one's roots." I took the name from the Okinawan word *nendukuruu*, meaning "a house that shelters the roots of one's clan members' souls." The word appealed to me because, as someone who left his native village for Tokyo and whose eyes had been opened by the study of European culture there, I had rediscovered—through my encounter with Okinawa—my own forest home, the fertile ground in which my writing has developed.

And now, as I approach sixty and look back on my career, I realize that everything I have written has been, in one way or another, an extrapolation of the two novels I have just discussed. The baby with the deformity was in reality my son, the fact of whose birth has overshadowed my life and writing. Over the years, I have often written on the theme of living with his mental handicap, and this same theme also informs my writing on Hiroshima and Nagasaki. I have tried to define the meaning that the experience of these two cities has for people in Japan and elsewhere, and I have been involved in activities associated with what I have written on this subject; but my fundamental perspective has always been that of the parent of a handicapped child. This is the experience that influences everything I write and everything I do. Thus, for example, my realization that life with a mentally handicapped child has the power to heal the wounds that family members inflict on one another led me to the more recent insight that the victims and survivors of the atomic bombs have the same sort of power to heal all of us who live in this nuclear age. This thought seems almost self-evident when one sees the survivors of Hiroshima and Nagasaki, by now frail and elderly, speaking up and taking an active part in the movement to abolish all nuclear weapons.

They are, to me, the embodiment of a prayer for the healing of our society, indeed the planet as a whole.

As for the theme of Japan's peripheral cultures which I dealt with in *The Silent Cry*, this too has featured in many of my other novels, where I have often portrayed groups independent of, or even in opposition to, the main Tokyo-centered culture. In the world of the novel, I have repeatedly tried to picture a village culture rooted in a cosmology that revolves around the cycle of life, death, and rebirth. This has been my way of resisting, on a mythological level, the homogenizing, centristic culture that has exerted its influence even over my own home in Shikoku. If you read my *M/T to mori no fushigi no monogatari*, which has been translated into Swedish and French, you will see that this novel, with others like it, is a record of my attempts to develop a model for this cultural alternative.

Japan's emperor system, which had apparently lost its social and political influence after the defeat in the Pacific War, is beginning to flex its muscles again, and in some respects it has already recouped much of its lost power—with two differences: first, the Japanese today will not accept the prewar ideology-cum-theology that held the emperor to be both absolute ruler and living deity. Nevertheless, imperial rites performed quite recently were done in such a manner as to impress upon us that the emperor's lineage can be traced to a deity; I am referring here to the rituals associated with the present emperor's enthronement and the so-called Great Thanksgiving Service that followed it. These ceremonies provoked little objection from either the government or the people, indeed most Japanese seemed to take it all very much for granted.

The second difference from the prewar situation is that the emperor is no longer the supreme commander of Japan's military forces. Under the present constitution, the so-called Self-Defense Forces should not even exist, yet Japan's military buildup has been enormous. The conservative party, perpetually in power, controls these forces and conducts itself as if the holy nimbus of the emperor were shining from behind it. This has been the state of affairs throughout the postwar years, and it can be thought of as the cause of one of the most sensational events of that period: the suicide of Yukio Mishima.

Mishima committed harakiri after calling for a coup d'état by the unconstitutional Self-Defense Forces, which he could not bear to see relegated to a status that virtually denied their very existence. He wanted to restore them to their role as the emperor's army, just as he wanted to restore the emperor himself to his place at the center of Japanese culture. The emperor at the heart of things —that was the core of Mishima's philosophy, but it was a philosophy founded on his own very peculiar ideas of traditional culture, and it served him and his kind alone. There is a wide range of opinion regarding the emperor system in Japan today, but it is alarming to see it regaining any popular support, for it has the kind of power that tends to override differing views.

In such an environment, I suspect that my novels may fall further out of the mainstream, insofar as they are based on folktales and mythology that pose a direct challenge to the emperor system. I do not mind this, however, since alienation from such a system can only help outline my literary microcosm even more sharply. I suppose my only regret is that my writing, in the sense that it is an act of resistance against reactionary tendencies in postwar Japan, has not had sufficient power to push back a rising tide of conformity.

As I said a moment ago, the world today is undergoing a major transition, and Japan, too, is in the midst of change. So, with some urgency, I find myself trying to answer a question that I believe all writers are asking: what is the role of a writer in times like these? What can our words accomplish? For my own part, I trust that the discussions I will have with the writers and students of Scandinavia will help me find an answer. That is why I have come here.

ON MODERN
AND CONTEMPORARY
JAPANESE LITERATURE

Wheatland Conference on Literature

San Francisco, 1990

odern Japanese literature can be said to have started with Japan's "modernization," that is, with the Meiji Restoration of 1868. This marked a new departure for the country, emerging from a feudal system into that of a nation-state centered on the absolute authority of the emperor. It involved more than just internal political reform; rather, the Restoration placed Japan in an international context. In this way, as regards both domestic and foreign affairs, the country underwent a great development, and faced a great crisis. Intellectuals of the time recognized the need for a narrative that would give the Japanese of this new age a voice of their own, and tried to create one. In this was the beginning of what can be called modern Japanese literature.

The pioneers of this literature were intellectuals, then, who were on a mission, yet who all possessed a language and a sensibility grounded on their education in the Chinese classics. To this they added other studies, about the literatures of Russia, Germany, France, and England, for example. They personally made translations of European works, and used them as a medium by which to create a narrative for the new age, having severed their ties with the established literary convention. They included intellectuals like Shimei Futabatei, who mastered Russian literature; Ogai Mori, who studied German and French; and Soseki Natsume, well versed in English writing. Thus there exists in Japan a line of narrative writing, extending back over a hundred years, that connects the work of these Meiji intellectuals with contemporary writers.

The modern nation-state of Japan continues to mark the passage of time by using names for eras whose currency holds good in Japan alone, names such as Meiji (1868–1912), Taisho (1912–1925), and Showa (1925–1989). And the Showa Emperor's death in 1989 revealed the power of this metaphorical system, wherein the names given to eras change with the passing of an emperor, resulting in a widely shared impression among the general public that a distinct period had come to an end. The end of Showa was especially significant because this era lasted longer than any other since the country's modernization, but also because it was marked by the most profound and complex changes.

What came to an end? By general account, a period of sixty-four years that witnessed the rise and fall of fascism; the invasion of China and the consequent Pacific War; the defeat and, at the core of the devastation, the atomic bomb; the recovery, the country built anew on the scorched earth; and economic prosperity. Another, minority account simply equates the end of the Showa era with the end of the postmodern.

When I think again of "Showa" in relation to contemporary writing or in the broader context of the connection between the establishment of a modern nation-state and the birth of modern writing in the nineteenth century, it seems symbolic that the writer Shohei Ooka died just before the Showa Emperor. And, bearing in mind the key role that writers and intellectuals played in this process, it seems particularly telling that the book Ooka produced at the very end of his life was a compilation of critical essays on the Meiji writer Soseki Natsume. Ooka, so fully representative of the writing of our time, continued up to the end to look back to Soseki with abiding admiration. "Once it had gained a hold on him," Ooka writes, "he shuttled pathologically between the West and Japan. As a literary phenomenon of the rarest kind the life of Soseki is inspiring." Although he was a Meiji writer it was not until 1925, the first year of the Showa period, that a range of Soseki's works became available in popular paperback editions, and thus was widely distributed. From then until the end of Showa, Soseki was the author most often read by a cross-section of the Japanese people. Looking back as far as the Meiji Restoration, and considering the totality of Japan's modernization through to the present, one can only answer the question "Who is Japan's national writer?" by giving Soseki Natsume's name.

Like most of his later fiction, *Sorekara* (translated as *And Then*), which he wrote in 1909, is a portrait of the Tokyo bourgeoisie of the time, and, through the voice of his intellectual hero, he delivered an attack on current cultural values, what one might call a critique of national identity, or *nihonjinron*. Modernization had brought Japan into contact with the West, and, on its victory in the Russo-Japanese War, the people of Japan fell captive to a desire—stimulated by the outside world—for material gains. At the same time, moral urgencies declined. Soseki's criticism, however, was not just leveled at Japan's economic pursuit of the West; he criticized the basic conditions of life as well (like the shabbiness of human dwellings), which had actually deteriorated in the process of modernization.

Like Soseki, who was deeply read in English literature, Ooka was familiar with foreign writing, especially with French literature. Moreover, Ooka had an encounter with the West—specifically America—far more intense than anything Soseki experienced, since he was taken prisoner by U.S. forces in the Philippines. From the defeat in the Pacific War through to the economic boom of the 1980s (which had not figured in any of Soseki's prophecies for Japan's future), Ooka was the writer and intellectual who was most representative of the time, whose cultural criticism was most trusted. That Ooka continued to write about Soseki must surely have been because in the 1980s he found himself in a position similar to Soseki's regarding his awareness that moral issues were being neglected while material desires were being stoked by the "outside." (It is well known that some of the greatest consumers of Western brand-name goods are young Japanese.) Similarly, too, despite the reach of Japan's economic might into the international arena, domestic living conditions remained shabby, especially in a large city like Tokyo, which was far easier to live in in Soseki's day.

One can say that from Soseki through Ooka, writing by and for intellectuals (whose education was based on a study of the West) represents a consistent lineage spanning a century of literary history. Yet it was in the period after the defeat—the era of the "postwar school" of literature—that the character of "intellectual writing" surfaced most clearly. And because Shohei Ooka was most representative of these writers, we can further say that the spirit of postwar literature remained an active force and a concrete presence until Ooka died at the end of the 1980s.

By 1945, the atomic bombing had reduced the cities of Hiroshima and Nagasaki to cinders, but this was also the fate of Tokyo and other urban areas. The whole country suffered food shortages. Yet, for the first time, freedom of expression was established and guaranteed, and, with it, previously suppressed literary energy burst forth. The leading figures on the postwar literary scene undertook an intensive reappraisal of their own society in the wake of all the misery it had caused in Asia. The years between 1945 and the economic growth of the sixties was a period marked by the fact that, while people had the greatest difficulty satisfying their material needs, the moral issues they found addressed in the literature of the time were at their highest tide.

Many postwar writers, as demonstrated by their participation in the broad-based movement opposing the U.S.–Japan Security Treaty in the 1960s, shared progressive political views. In reaction to these prevailing views, Yukio Mishima, who belonged to the same generation, for a combination of personal and political reasons (which became all the more evident in the behavior that marked the last years of his life) practiced and proclaimed a distinctive brand of nationalism. Yet although Mishima and his literary counterparts were moving in opposite ideological directions, in their common desire for moral values to take precedence over material ones they together reveal a distinguishing trait in the writing of those years, a characteristic of serious literature going back to Soseki.

As might be expected, this "intellectual writing" depended on an intellectual readership. Postwar literature in particular, representing as it did proof of a new freedom of expression, attracted intelligent readers of all kinds. Holding debates with writers on common themes, political theorists, economists, and scientists also contributed to the literary magazines of the day and helped to arouse the interest of a thoughtful readership.

Yet it must be said that as the devastation of the immediate postwar period gave way to the recovery of the 1950s, and then to a period of economic expansion pointing toward the manifest prosperity of the boom years, by degrees literature lost its intellectual appeal for much of the population. Consider for a moment the publishing industry. It is true that five literary monthlies continue to appear. In them we still find short stories—a genre central to the character of Japanese literature. It is a common practice as well for many long novels to appear first in this format, in monthly installments. Yet at present all these literary magazines are operating in the red. The losses are covered in two ways: by the successful sales of the book that comes out of the installments and is produced—as though from the same womb—by the same publishing company; and significantly by the company publishing a good deal of sheer entertainment, including comic books—the ubiquitous *manga*.

And so serious literature and a literary readership have gone into a chronic decline, while a new tendency has emerged over the last several years. This strange new phenomenon is largely an economic one, reflected in the fact that the novels of certain young writers like Haruki Murakami and

Banana Yoshimoto each sells several hundred thousand copies. It is possible that the recent sales of the books produced by these two authors alone are greater than those of all other living novelists combined. Here we see Japan's economic boom making itself felt in the literary market. In contrast to much postwar writing which fictionalized the actual experience of writers and readers who, as twenty- and thirty-year-olds, had known war, Murakami and Yoshimoto convey the experience of a youth politically uninvolved or disaffected, content to exist within a late adolescent or post-adolescent subculture. And their work evokes a response bordering on adulation in their young readers. But it is too early to predict where this trend will lead as they grow older. Will the audience brought together and cultivated by people like Murakami and Yoshimoto come more generally to be the mainstay of Japanese fiction? Or will this readership, along with its favored writers, all vanish with its own subculture?

In fairness to Yoshimoto's recent work, it should be said that it does faithfully reflect the habits and attitudes of the young in Japan, a youth culture which on the surface resembles its counterparts in New York or Paris. Her fiction is at least an unselfconscious expression of her own generation. But in the case of Murakami, a writer in his forties and in that sense a generation older than Yoshimoto, we have an exceedingly self-conscious representation of contemporary cultural habits. Murakami is also a conscientious reader of modern American fiction as well as a translator who has rendered American minimalism in an impressive Japanese narrative style. In this respect, he represents an "intellectual writer" along the lines of Soseki and Ooka. Yet Murakami, in capturing an extremely wide and avid readership, has accomplished what had hitherto been beyond the reach of other genuinely intellectual writers, however much they drew on the contemporary writing of Europe and America for ideological or stylistic inspiration.

Even so, while Yoshimoto and Murakami are conspicuous surface figures on the literary scene, I would draw your attention to another new tendency, which exists perhaps as an undercurrent. A number of serious contemporary writers, even as they were experiencing a cold winter of dwindling sales, were storing up a sense of the real power and efficacy of literature, which many of their predecessors did not possess. And in their hands, if they continue to work with determination, a broadbased intellectual audience may well return to them before too long. Among those I have in mind is Kobo Abe, one of the first major figures to emerge after the war, who works on a level consciously detached from Japanese tradition, and continues to construct fictional worlds which, however abstract they may seem, are nevertheless replete with Abe's personal but authentic view of contemporary life. Also Yoshikichi Furui, ten years younger than Abe, has applied his imagination to the task of connecting the interior landscape of an alienated citizenry, living in an urban, mass society, with the sense of life and death held by Japanese of ancient or medieval times.

Among even younger writers, I would mention Kenji Nakagami, whose writing has taken on a density and texture over the years, as he has given shape to a territory on the margins of Japanese life, that of a former outcast people, revealing their mythological dimensions. Nakagami's contemporary, Yuko Tsushima, has succeeded in creating a narrative style capable of portraying women, after over a hundred years of "modernization," on both a universal level and the level of daily life. And Masahiko Shimada, still in his early twenties, has begun to produce a vivid fictional account, using a parodistic style edged with a sharp critical intent, of the same generation whose cultural attitudes are transcribed in the work of Murakami and Yoshimoto.

What are the historical, social issues that have generated this new undercurrent in Japanese literature? Now that Showa has come to an end, where is serious writing headed? Our answer should take account of how modernization and modern literature came about, from the Meiji Restoration onward.

Consider the fact that throughout most of this historical period, the Japanese existed as strangers for the West. They were a little-known people whose true character, it was believed, could never be comprehended. For America, Japan came to be the enemy. Now again, in the wake of Japan's prosperity and the creation of an international information network, the Japanese are being placed in full view of Americans and Europeans as competitive traders. And the notion of the inscrutable Japanese character still lingers. I even wonder if the image now being presented to the world isn't of a people more unfathomable than ever.

Japanese writers and intellectuals need to respond to this crisis and, using a range of strategies, compel a majority of politicians, bureaucrats, and business leaders to put forward a more accurate image of Japan and its people. What Europeans and Americans should clearly see is a Japan possessing a view of the world richly shaped by both traditional and foreign cultural elements, and a will to work as a cooperative member of the world community, to make an independent and distinctive contribution to the environment of our shared planet. Japanese intellectuals should feel the urgency of achieving this all the more, given the recent dramatic changes in East–West relations.

Contemporary writing must respond to this

sense of crisis and mission. Only then will the Japanese novel be able to claim the full attention of an informed readership. As one contemporary writer, I want to work toward this end.

Japan's modernization reveals the history of an Asian country that sought to extricate itself from Asia and become a European-style nation. This was accompanied by a tendency in modern Japanese literature to focus on writing in Europe, Russia, and America. Even today, Japanese writers look to the West, which now includes Eastern Europe and Latin America. Yet with the new literary movements in China and Korea, certain young Japanese writers and critics have begun to call for a serious study of Asian literature. This strikes me as one possible direction Japanese literature may be heading in. And this would lead us directly away from a narrow, aggressive nationalism, toward a more open future.

JAPAN'S
DUAL IDENTITY:
A WRITER'S DILEMMA

Duke University, 1986

Translated by Kunioki Yanagishita

I come to you today as one Japanese writer who feels that Japanese literature may be decaying. A confession like this by a writer from the third world will undoubtedly disappoint an audience that is expecting a genuine "challenge," given the theme of our discussion: "The Challenge of Third World Culture." There are reasons, however, why I readily accept the part of disappointing clown; and these have to do with an element in the Japanese nation and its people that makes them unwilling to accept the fact that they are members of the third world and reluctant to play their role accordingly. Japan appeared on the international scene as a third-world nation in about 1868. Ever since, in the process of modernizing, it has been blatantly hostile to its fellow third-world nations in Asia, as evidenced by its annexation of Korea and its war of aggression against China. Japan's hostility toward its neighbors continues even today.

The destruction we wrought upon China during the invasion was so great that what was destroyed can never be restored or compensated for. However, even now, more than forty years after the end of the war, I do not think that we have done enough to make amends where they can be made—either economically or culturally. Nor is the annexation of Korea in 1910 a bygone matter when one considers the discriminatory status imposed on some six hundred thousand Korean residents in Japan at present. Furthermore, when one sees our government supporting a South Korean regime that oppresses citizens aspiring to democracy in that nation, it becomes clear that Japan is in fact one of the powers that oppresses the third world. This, surely, is the national image of Japan held not only by those who seek democracy in South Korea but by democratic forces throughout Asia, which makes me more than ever determined to listen with undivided attention to the criticism of my colleagues here, and especially to the participant from the

Philippines, Kidlat Tahimik. Japan has betrayed those who aspire to freedom in third-world countries, and has often been an aggressor toward those nations among which it should count itself. The burden of that knowledge weighs heavily on me.

What, then, is the image of Japan in the eyes of the industrialized nations? If, during my stay here in the United States, I am welcomed by neutral smiles, it is because I am an engineer who designs products that are not very competitive in the international market: I produce novels and not automobiles, TV sets, or audio equipment. Being such a person, I can remain indifferent to whatever favors the happy users of Japanese products may ply me with, or to the hostility with which workers who have to compete with Japanese companies may greet me. Nevertheless, when I compare this visit with my first one twenty years ago, I—by the mere fact of being Japanese—cannot help feeling a sense of crisis, one that I always feel while in Japan, but made much clearer, and felt more acutely, over here.

This sense of crisis comes from living in a country that, though an economic giant with a huge trade surplus, is dependent on imports for most of its food and resources. Ours is a nation where the livelihood of its people would be devastated if the balance of imports and exports were disrupted. I feel the anxiety of someone living in a country that, in the process of rising to the status of a technologically advanced nation, has spread pollution everywhere and is unable to find an answer to its own environmental problems. I feel the danger of living in a country that, though it experienced the bombings of Hiroshima and Nagasaki, is now run by a government that supports the American SDI program, thereby helping spread the myth of nuclear deterrence in the Far East.

Because of its wealth, Japan is now considered a member of the advanced nations, but it is not an independent country with plans of its own—plans to establish world peace. I feel the misgivings of a citizen in a nation of self-satisfied people—as demonstrated by the recent landslide victory of the party led by Prime Minister Nakasone, President Reagan's good friend—and tremble with fear when I think that the people on those islands in the Far East are heading for destruction without knowing it. But in a few weeks' time I will have to go back to those islands, to be lost in the crowd there again.

This is the frame of reference of my talk—one that may at times be confusing, because I speak from a standpoint of twofold or perhaps threefold ambiguities. Still, for my own sake I hope to be able to overcome these ambiguities; I also like to imagine that at some future date a form of Japanese culture might make a special contribution to the cultures of its Asian neighbors. Toward this end, I will present these ambiguities as they really are, and would like to ask my fellow panelists to guide me out of them.

As I mentioned earlier, I suspect that Japanese literature is decaying. That is to say, I have good reason to believe that the Japanese are losing their power to produce an active model of life in the present and for the future. I suspect that modern Japanese culture is losing its vitality, and that we are seeing, as a consequence, the waning of its literature. Literature no longer seems able to capture the attention of the younger generation, which usually responds so sensitively to new cultural developments—a fact, I believe, that is already common knowledge in cultural journalism. And this is an ominous phenomenon, threatening not merely cultural journalism itself but Japanese culture as a whole.

It is not unusual for Kurt Vonnegut to introduce Japanese figures into his compassionate but apocalyptic pictures of the future world. One such work depicts a city destroyed by a neutron bomb: a city in which human life has been extinguished but where the machinery of the highly mechanized Matsushita and Honda factories is still in motion. The roof of one of the buildings is painted to resemble Mt. Fuji, and the city, apparently somewhere in the American Midwest, becomes a metaphor for the Japanese archipelago. I admit that I, too, can imagine a scenario in which Japanese culture, after losing the capacity to create a human model for the future, withers and dies, leaving behind nothing that moves but a few objects like cars, TVs, and microcomputers—and a younger generation taking no notice of the oddity of the situation.

But I want to look more closely at the signs foretelling this decline. A characteristic lexical item employed by Japanese writers is the term *junbungaku*, which in English might be translated as "sincere literature." It was only after the Meiji Restoration that a modern literature, with strong European influences, developed in my country. The precursory treatise that provided the rationale for literature in Japan was Shoyo Tsubouchi's *Shosetsu shinzui* (*The Essence of the Novel*) published in 1885—seventeen years after the Restoration. By then, Tokoku Kitamura, a pioneer in modern Japanese romanticism and a keen student of his times, had already started to use the term *junbungaku*. He wrote that certain people seemed intent on "crushing *junbungaku* with the iron hammer of Historical Theory." The term as Tokoku used it was antithetical to the sciences of philosophy and history with which the Japanese of the early and mid-Meiji era, by borrowing European ideas, strove to establish the spirit of modernization. But in its present usage it refers to something different: literature that has, as it were, passively cut itself off from the products published by the mass media; in other words, literature that is not "popular" or "mundane."

To spend time discussing what constitutes "serious literature" may seem a bit ridiculous to a non-Japanese audience, but I do so in order to confirm my own identity as a Japanese writer. The role of literature—insofar as man is obviously a historical being—is to create a model of a contemporary age which encompasses past and future, a model of the people living in that age as well. In Japan, where the history of modern and contemporary literature spans a period of over a hundred years, there have been a few men of letters whose works surpassed their times. But, for a short period beginning immediately after the Pacific War, there were also a number of writers who collectively, as a definite literary movement, provided a comprehensive image of their times. This new literary phenomenon, especially during the first ten years, had a vital impact, and continued to thrive as long as these writers continued to write, even amidst various other literary trends.

It is difficult to say exactly when this movement ended, but specific works such as Shohei

Ooka's "The Battle of Leyte" (1969) and Taijun Takeda's "Mount Fuji Sanatorium" (1971) suggest that the date might be set somewhere around 1970. That was also the year Yukio Mishima committed suicide after calling for an uprising by members of the Self-Defense Forces, the de facto armed forces of Japan. Although his writing was an attempt to create a different model from that presented by his contemporaries, he too can be counted, from a broader perspective, as one of the postwar literati.

Theirs was a literature that set out to deal squarely with the needs of intellectuals, and it did in fact win firm support from them in various fields which went beyond the narrow realm that Tokoku championed in defiance of philosophy and history in order to assert his raison d'être, when *junbungaku* was still in an embryonic stage. Calling desperately for the protection of *junbungaku*, he built a fence around a lot next to the buildings erected by the philosophy-and-history architects who had imported know-how and material from Europe, so that later he and his associates would at least have something on which to build their own house. But it can rightly be said that Tokoku's labors in mid-Meiji eventually bore fruit in the form of postwar literature.

How was it possible for postwar writers to accomplish all they did? The feat can be attributed to historical pressures. The "postwar school" started to publish its works within two or three years after Japan's defeat. Yutaka Haniya's "Ghosts," Hiroshi Noma's "Dark Pictures," Yukio Mishima's "Cigarette," Taijun Takeda's *Saishi kajin*, and Haruo Umezaki's *Sakurajima* all appeared within a year or so after the war. (In Mishima's case, however, *Confessions of a Mask*, published in 1949, is more characteristic of postwar literature than "Cigarette.") The year 1947 saw the publication of Rinzo Shiina's "Midnight Banquet." A year after that came Toshio Shimao's "Island's End," Shohei Ooka's "Prisoner of War," and Kobo Abe's "Road Sign at the End of the Street"—and here already we have the whole array of postwar literati. These were people who had to endure silence while fascism prevailed prior to and during the war years. Their pent-up frustrations were released in a burst of activity that formed them as intellectuals. On the day of Japan's defeat, their ages ranged from twenty to thirty-six, Mishima being the youngest and Shohei Ooka the oldest.

During the years of intellectual suppression—that is, the immediate prewar period and the war itself—Haniya was exposed to Marxism through the peasant movement, Noma through the movement to liberate former outcast communities, some of whose members continue to be discriminated against. Takeda and Shiina, while respectively a student and a laborer, suffered oppression for having participated in leftist activities. Ooka was taken prisoner by the U.S. forces. Noma, Takeda, and Umezaki were drafted. Shimao was a kamikaze pilot awaiting orders for a suicide attack when news of the defeat reached him. And neither Abe nor Mishima was free from the turmoil in the colonies or from the effects of student mobilization.

In addition to their common experience of harsh reality, each of these writers was either a researcher in some special field of interest or at least a very careful reader. Haniya and Shiina studied Dostoyevsky; Takeda read Lu Xun; Noma immersed himself in French symbolism; and Ooka read Stendhal. In fact, all the postwar writers were young intellectuals who had endeavored to establish their identities by absorbing European literature. Unable to express themselves during the war years, they honed their minds and lived with a spirit of defiance toward the war being fought by the fascist government that ruled them. Postwar literature was simply a kind of simultaneous outburst of self-expression once freedom came.

The defeat in the Pacific War, which brought about a decisive period of transition among Japan's writers, was, needless to say, the most important event in the history of the country's development since the mid-nineteenth century. For Japan, which had pursued modernization so avidly and had dared to compete with the imperialist powers of Western Europe, the defeat was nothing less than the confrontation of a total impasse for an imperialistically underdeveloped nation. The surrender also led to an examination of elements askew in Japanese culture and tradition from premodern days. Moreover, the defeat spurred reform which in turn gave impetus to third-world-oriented liberation movements both within and outside the nation.

If one were to look for a metaphor for this situation in literature, one might choose Dickens's novels, which are studded with "units" of differing significance. As we read, the "units" progress along the paths Dickens plots for each of them. When the novel is completed, each unit is illuminated by a retrospective light which reveals its full meaning. The individual units are already alive and have significance in and of themselves within the story as it progresses, yet the light cast by the denouement shows us not a contradiction but a new interpretation. In a similiar manner, the various units that were part of the "plot" of modernization beginning with the Meiji Restoration took on a dual meaning with the defeat, that light shining back on things from the finale. Thus the Japanese, in losing the Pacific War, saw for the first time the entire picture of the modernization of a nation called Japan; and it was postwar literature that most sensitively and candidly painted that picture of Japan and its people.

On an international level, Japan's modernization took the form of the annexation of Korea, an invasion of China, and incursions into other regions of Asia. Intellectuals who witnessed these events and the downfall of their country's territorial expansion, wrote of what they saw in various ways. Takeda and Hotta told of their experiences in China. Noma and Ooka wrote about what happened to them in the Philippines. The work of those Japanese writers who saw Japan as an aggressor was complemented by the literary activities of Korean nationals living in Japan; and Korean writers themselves, writing in Japanese, have delved into Japan's colonial rule over the Korean peninsula, a matter which has ramifications even today. Okinawa, under the Ryukyu Empire, long maintained an independent culture with its own characteristic political system and cosmology. After being taken over by Japan, however, it was victimized in the process of Japan's drive to modernize itself to a far greater extent than any other prefecture. The fact that Okinawa became the sole battlefield of the Pacific War on Japanese soil speaks for itself. The islands were totally devastated, and even after the signing of the peace treaty, they remained under the control of U.S. forces for many years. Still, Okinawa has managed to accomplish its own reconstruction, and because of this experience, it has preserved a certain independent identity.

The identity of the people of Okinawa is a product of their realistic ideas, efforts, and cultural traditions; and we can find in this identity direct and important clues for the Japanese in their search for a life style that does not pose a threat to other Asian nations. Similar clues are offered by those writers who have looked for ways to recover from the experiences of the Hiroshima and Nagasaki bombings. These are people deeply involved in the movement that seeks the enactment of the A-Bomb Victims' Relief Law and the eradication of all nuclear weapons. They look squarely at the destructive impasse to which Japan's efforts to catch up with the West brought us. It is here that we can find for ourselves a principle according to which Japan could live as part of Asia in this nuclear age. Whether or not this principle is adopted should be the basis on which the country is judged over the last forty years.

If we add to the list of postwar writers the name of Tamiki Hara, who wrote about his experiences as an A-bomb victim in Hiroshima and who chose to commit suicide as soon as a new conflict—the Korean War—broke out, it will become that much clearer that the preoccupation of postwar writers was to examine, with all the force of their imagination, what, in its pursuit of modernization, Japan had done to Asia and to the vulnerable elements in its own society, how the impasse could only have led to its defeat, and what means of resuscitation were possible for the nation after its death as a state.

It is also worth examining how the postwar writers dealt with the problem of the emperor system, for this was the cultural and political axle on which the program of modernization turned. One of the conditions necessary to maintain this program was national unity. Thus, until the defeat in 1945, the emperor was made the absolute figurehead and essentially a living deity, and progress was pursued under the pretext of his inviolable authority. At the beginning of the following year, however, the emperor issued a proclamation stating that he was not divine, a statement endorsed by General MacArthur. (The fact that soon afterward another "emperor"—a certain "Emperor Kumazawa"—appeared, claiming to be the descendant of an emperor in the Middle Ages, is one indication of the sort of diversity and energy this released.) But the Japanese Imperial Army, which invaded various regions of Asia, was first and foremost the emperor's army. In Okinawa, the only part of Japan on which any battle was fought, thousands of its citizens died; and commentators have claimed that the suffering of the Okinawans was made even worse by their sense of loyalty to the emperor, a loyalty stronger than that of Japanese on the mainland, since they took special pride in the fact that, after the Meiji Restoration, they became the emperor's subjects for the first time in their history.

The aim of the postwar writers was to "relativize" the value of the emperor, who had had absolute power, and to free the Japanese from the curse of a system that had haunted their minds, even at the subconscious level. To take one example: if the emperor stood at the very top of the structural hierarchy, Hiroshi Noma depicted the bottom, the former outcasts for whom he had been working since before the war. Noma continued to write about them even after the period of postwar literature was widely considered to be over. *Ring of Youth*, a novel on which he spent many years, was completed a year after Mishima's suicide. The work was about a show of force by members of these communities, which proved victorious. Their success was only short-lived, but the mere fact that Noma attributed a victory to those who had been most oppressed was in itself meaningful.

By contrast, Mishima's call for a coup d'état at the compound of the Self-Defense Forces in Ichigaya and his subsequent suicide were a theatrical performance. In his later years Mishima's political, moral, and aesthetic principles centered on his deep regret over the emperor's proclaiming he was not a deity but a human being. Mishima's suicide is an incident that is hard to erase from one's memory, something he himself apparently hoped to ensure, since he seems to have left behind a baleful ghost that appears whenever Japan encounters a political crisis. This is one of the reasons why I set 1970 as the year in which the curtain came down on postwar literature—a literature which, in 1946, was begun as a means of giving vent to cultural energies that had been suppressed since prewar days. And when I refer to signs that Japanese literature is decaying, I am referring to nothing other than the loss of this postwar literature with its unique status in our culture, the power it possessed to enlighten Japan and its people.

What, then, is the situation of serious literature in the latter half of the 1980s? Young intellectuals who respond quickly to intellectual fads say that *junbungaku* is already dead, or that it is about to breathe its last. They believe that, although there may still be some literary activity shoved away in some bleak corner of journalism where the survivors are barely making a living, the latter will sooner or later fade away in the natural course of events. This group of young intellectuals is composed of critics, playwrights, screenwriters, and introducers of various new cultural theories from

America and Europe. It even includes writers whose works are firmly outside the realm of *junbungaku*, as well as journalists in various fields and a group that nowadays enjoys the greatest popularity among the younger generation: the copywriters of commercial messages. One might also add almost all the "cultural heroes" of Japan's grotesquely bloated consumer society. Lack of activity in the field of *junbungaku* can be substantiated objectively when we compare the volume of its publications with that of other types of literature, such as popular historical novels, science fiction, mysteries, and various nonfiction genres. Although, obviously, the prewar and war years provide no basis for comparison, never have there been so many publications in Japan as in the past forty years. The number of serious literary works, however, has decreased as the number of other publications has continued to grow. Moreover, there is not one work of *junbungaku* to be found in the 1985 list of the ten best-selling Japanese books in either fiction or nonfiction.

Amidst this trend, Haruki Murakami, a writer born after the war, is said by some to be attracting new readers to *junbungaku*. It is clear, however, that Murakami's target lies outside this sphere, and deliberately so. There is nothing that directly links Murakami with postwar literature of the 1946–1970 period. If I may be allowed a possibly hasty comment here, I believe that no revival of *junbungaku* will be possible unless ways are found to fill the wide gap that exists between him and pre-1970 writing.

Another indication of the long downward path *junbungaku* is taking is the prolonged business slump of the literary monthlies, magazines peculiar to the local literary scene which helped nurture and develop a form of short story unique to Japanese literature. I am sure that these literary magazines are of little concern to the young intellectuals who are now the vanguard of Japan's consumer society. However, looking back on the first ten years after the war, such magazines, together with a number of general interest publications, played an important role in maintaining high cultural standards. Almost all of the representative literary works—the ones I mentioned earlier— were first published there; yet now these same magazines are treated with derision by young intellectuals, who regard their heyday as a myth, if they think about them at all.

I must also mention here the season of "intellectuality" that flourished in the latter half of the 1970s and lasted through the first half of the 1980s, a period that coincides with the decline of *junbungaku*. Based on new cultural theories, all of which were imported from Europe and America, its impact was so strong that it overwhelmed intellectual journalism. Here we should not forget that the intellectuals who established postwar literature and had been educated before or during the war years had acquired a certain cultural sophistication. Almost all of them were strongly influenced by cultural theories from Western Europe or from Russia via Western Europe, which was only natural since the eyes and ears of the Japanese intelligentsia have been directed toward the West since the Meiji Restoration. Even a writer like Rinzo Shiina, who spent his youth as a laborer instead of pursuing higher education, prepared for his literary career through his involvement in the Marxist movement; and, oddly enough, what converted him from Marxism was his encounter with Dostoyevsky. Taijun Takeda, on the other hand, studied Chinese classical literature while Japan was rapidly preparing to invade China. Takeda was greatly influenced by Lu Xun, but for him, too, Dostoyevsky was a thinker without whom he would not have been able to establish his own literary identity.

It is from these writers and from others who had been influenced by European literature and thought that the "postwar school" was born. Their methodology for delving into Japanese traditional thought and culture was also European, a fact that is confirmed when we examine how Masao Maruyama established his school of Japanese political thought. Maruyama was a prominent contemporary of the postwar writers. By studying those writers, Maruyama in turn opened up new horizons for them. Thus the predilection for European culture that prevailed among the intellectuals who were in the vanguard of Japan's modernization carried over to the generation that came after them and continued to characterize their thinking.

The Mexican thinker, Octavio Paz, marks 1968 as an extremely significant year and calls our attention to the protest movements and riots that occurred in Prague, Chicago, Paris, Tokyo, Belgrade, Rome, Mexico City, and Santiago. Student riots raged everywhere like a medieval plague, affecting people regardless of religious affiliation or social class. Because the riots were spontaneous, they were all the more widespread, and Paz analyzed their significance in the light of the situation in which all technologically advanced societies, East or West, found themselves. In Japan, it was the time when the United Red Army, formed three years after the Tokyo riots, marched down the path toward its own annihilation. The bodies of numerous Red Army members executed in cold blood by their own comrades were dug up after the Asama Mountain villa incident of 1972, a year that happens to coincide with the approximate time when the "postwar school" came to a close. As if in reaction to this period of political action, the new generation of the 1970s and 1980s tended to be antipolitical. What Paz pointed out about identical subcultural trends having global horizontal ties held true also in Tokyo.

It should be borne in mind that these events prepared the way for the recent fashion for bringing in new cultural ideas from the West. Speaking for myself, as one writer, I have a high opinion of the various schools of thought springing from structuralism, for they gave a powerful stimulus to the field of literature. I will elaborate below on one example of the effectiveness of its introduction. So influential has it been that I am even tempted to make a comparison between the diverse influences of the structuralism-based cultural ideas of the 1970s and 1980s and the effect Marxism had on Japanese minds when it flourished for a short time before the war.

The influx of new cultural theories coming in the wake of structuralism was such that it appeared they would permeate the whole nation's intellectual climate. An excellent summary of these theories, *Structure and Power*, by a young scholar named Akira Asada, was read on university campuses everywhere. The book sold equally well outside academic circles and became one of the most widely read works since the war. It was by no means easy reading, but no serious publication of that period generated as much intellectual interest among the younger generation. There followed a time in which many new French cultural ideas—some of which came via America—were translated and introduced, including poststructuralism and postmodernism, particularly the work of Barthes, Foucault, Derrida, Lacan, Kristeva, and the Yale School of deconstructionists.

As far as translations are concerned, aside from works of mere journalistic faddishness, some projects representing real intellectual labor started to appear in the latter half of the 1980s. Nevertheless, by then, enthusiasm among the younger generation for this new wave of ideas had come to an end, as it had in the realm of intellectual journalism which had staged, directed, and transmitted it.

While all of this was taking place, I was already an older writer, and had never been part of the boom anyway; but as I stand amid the ruins of it—voluminous introductory works and translations—and look back on that period, I am struck by several things. First, that young Japanese intellectuals, true to our national character, analyzed and diachronically systematized the various structuralism-based theories and counterarguments in order to "accept" and—to use a term not usually considered its antonym—"discharge" those theories. To accept Foucault, Barthes had to be discharged. Only after Lacan was dismissed could Derrida be accepted—but merely to make room for the next new thinker. The shuttling of new cultural theories was, up to a point, an easy task for the introducers and translators who advocated their importation. Cultural heroes came and went. However, the curtain dropped on this period as soon as these advocates found there was no thinker or thought left for them to add to the conveyor belt from Europe and the States.

At the height of the ongoing process of accepting and discharging new theories, phrases such as "a performance of ideas" or "a playground of texts" came into common usage. These expressions seemed remarkably appropriate for those who could cope only passively with the kaleidoscope of ideas. Also, in this same period, a very Japanese

touch was added to the use of the prefix "post-."
By speaking of "poststructuralism" or "postmodernism," or of some theory that was yet to come and thus unimaginable (which seems self-evident, since all they did was passively accept and then discharge), these "performers of ideas" assumed optimistically that, when some cultural theory had been established, a new one could be made to follow it simply by adding the prefix "post-" to the existing one. As a consequence, many of these people must have been dismayed to find that some "post-" concept of theirs did not mean much since the concept itself meant nothing in the first place, and it would not surprise me if some of them felt impelled to take drastic measures—even self-deconstruction.

Secondly, despite this extraordinary fashion for importing new intellectual trends, almost no effort was made to analyze them carefully in terms of their application to the specific situation in Japan. Why then did they become so popular? Strange as it may seem, I believe it can be attributed mainly to a special characteristic which Japan's intellectual journalists developed soon after the Meiji Restoration. To put it bluntly, there has been, and still is, a tendency to think that an intellectual effort has been made merely by transplanting or translating new Western concepts into Japanese; and this belief is held by both the translators and those who read their translations.

Since the most important skills required in the task of introducing new cultural ideas were the ability to read the foreign language in which those thoughts were presented and to translate the works into Japanese, the spokesmen for these theories were often specialists in literature or languages. Even when one theory replaced another in rapid succession, however, the spokesmen themselves were not replaced, because they were not necessarily advocates—or critics, even—of what they spoke for. Thus a handful of literature and language specialists became the importers of things about which they themselves felt, at best, lukewarm. Obviously, the responsibility does not rest solely with these specialists. If the readers had read their summaries and translations in a way that enabled them to use the new cultural theories to interpret the reality of Japan, their understanding of these theories would have been raised to a higher level. Such an understanding might, in turn, have fostered an ability to offer some response to the source of those ideas. Nor would it have been possible for each new theory itself, or those who had a hand in introducing it in Japan, to remain free from criticism. But such was not the case. As soon as an introduction or translation was made, the one-way journey from abroad was completed; the process of "acceptance" and "discharge" was over. This is how the continual expectation of theoretical developments became a convention.

This tendency has produced another characteristic phenomenon in today's intellectual climate: namely, the absence of any effort to accept synchronically a variety of cultural theories. Never have we witnessed, in intellectual journalism in Japan, the synchronic existence of two opposing new schools of thought—for example, structuralism and deconstructionism—and the resulting combination of antagonism and complementarity, which can lead, in turn, to a mutual deepening of each. That is why—with the exception of the

architect Arata Isozaki, who in his work has substantiated his criticism of postmodernism—the
cultural anthropologist Masao Yamaguchi, the
forerunner among introducers of new cultural
theories, stands out as unique and is now being
reappraised. Yamaguchi, originally a specialist in
monarchism, with field-study experience in Nige-
ria, went against the general trend in his work
Periphery and Center, employing a structuralist
methodology to substantiate his unique cultural
interpretation of Japan's particular circumstances.
In discussing the importance of postwar literature,
his theory, together with its diverse implications,
has been extremely helpful in clarifying the significance of the emperor system. Yet his critics have
charged that he is mistaken in thinking that, in the
context of Japan, placing importance on peripheral
cultures and stimulating them would lead to a
reversal of the relationship between those cultures
and the central one. They asserted that stimulating
the periphery would merely establish a more solid
central authority, and that the ideas in his *Periphery and Center* were therefore reactionary. Their
accusation of a form of political short-circuiting

overlooked the fact that Yamaguchi's structuralism was scrupulously calculated to include a kind of implicit deconstructionism. His ideas were based on structuralist methodology, but because they coexisted from the outset with criticism based on deconstructive methodology, they gained in depth, and became more realistically valid. By citing various examples from Japanese mythology and from literature of the Middle Ages, Yamaguchi proved that despite the dichotomy between the central elite (the imperial family) and those who were driven onto the margins of society, the two often "blended together like fresh ink spots on blotting paper."

Although Yamaguchi's political thought overlaps with that of Yukio Mishima, the two point at diametrically opposite poles. Mishima, who lamented the fact that the emperor made his "Human Proclamation" after the defeat and who called for a military coup d'état, sought to establish the emperor system as an absolute cultural principle and in it find a paradigm for political unity among the Japanese. If, however, Yamaguchi's ideas as expounded in *Periphery and Center* were to activate the peripheral aspects of Japanese culture and this, in turn, were to lead to a strengthening of the center—namely, the emperor system—the resulting system would be one totally different from that advocated by Mishima. Yamaguchi's emperor system would never be the kind that might serve as an incentive for the Self-Defense Forces to carry out a coup d'état. His cultural theory, when reread in the light of contemporary reality, reveals nothing that can be thought liable to produce a political short-circuit or political retrogression. His unique "trickster" theory, too, is further evidence that his thinking leaves no room whatsoever for such criticism, stemming from uncompromising political ideologies. However, Yamaguchi's pioneering work, which led to the rise of other cultural theories, was not properly followed up by the introducers of these theories— the cultural heroes of the late 1970s and early 1980s—and this points to the heart of the problem under discussion.

I started my presentation by stating that Japanese literature is decaying and referred specifically to the "postwar school" of writers, who represent the highest level of writing since the onset of Japan's modernization. I also noted the obvious decline of Japanese literature at this highest level—termed *junbungaku*—and how cultural theories, which replaced *junbungaku* in capturing the minds of young intellectuals, came to be accepted and rejected in a manner characteristic of Japan. I believe that intelligent members of their generation during the late 1970s and early 1980s were keenly aware of the decline of Japanese literature and, on the rebound, fell head over heels for the new cultural fashions from Europe and America. So great was the number of commentaries and translations published each year that these seemed to outnumber new literary works. However, their enthusiasm was short-lived, coming and going like a passing craze. In the intellectual climate of the time, the new cultural theories, as one organic part of literature's decline, fell prey to the general tendency toward decay even faster than literature itself. The two phenomena, I feel— literature and its readers on the one hand, and cultural trends and the young intellectuals who accepted them on the other—should be viewed not in contrast but as one entity "blended together like fresh ink spots on blotting paper."

From a broader perspective, one can say that they were not truly intellectuals as such but merely young Japanese following a subcultural fad that swept through an average, urban consumer society. Moreover, if we were to extrapolate from the contention of sociologists—though one filled with contradictions when examined in the light of people's actual lives— that a middle-class consciousness is shared by the vast majority of the population, we can say that this phenomenon attests to the fact that, compared to their counterparts in the days of the student riots, young Japanese have become markedly more conservative. As political scientists have pointed out, this conservative trend among the younger generation in the large urban areas was an important factor in the recent landslide victory of the incumbent party. Other noticeable signs of this conservatism have started to appear in the big cities, where the bulk of the younger generation lives; and such signs will soon begin to crop up in smaller towns as well, since the members of their generation are linked by an urban subculture that spans the nation.

The problem here, in the context of our discussion, is that these young people, so closely conjoined subculturally on a nationwide level, are abandoning literature. Moreover, this is the same generation that abandoned the trend in new cultural theories almost as quickly as it embraced it. Akira Asada's *Structure and Power* was at one time such a fad on university campuses that it was even referred to as the "Asada phenomenon." But, unlike other fads adopted by the young which can sometimes lead to positive results, as actually happened in many countries after World War II, nothing of this kind occurred in Japan.

The postwar writers and their contemporary pioneers in cultural theory were people who had gone through the hardships of war. Being part of the younger generation themselves, they were able to produce works that had a positive influence on that generation, which was searching for a way to redefine itself in the midst of a society that had recently suffered defeat. It is thus that they were able to educate the youth of a generation that followed their own. Speaking for myself, it was the postwar writers who laid the foundations for my own writing. In the realm of politics, the conservative party has of course held a monopoly in the Diet for decades; but I believe that the generation of readers of postwar literature demonstrated its strength by casting enough votes for opposition-party members to keep the government in check. The popular movement in 1960 to protest the ratification of the new U.S.–Japan Security Treaty was one that had actively incorporated the opinions of the postwar writers and cultural theorists. It was a movement equally as powerful as, and more animated than, the progressive opposition parties and the labor unions. A comparison of the political and cultural situation of those years— twenty years ago—with that of today sheds light on exactly what has been lost and how we lost it. The light shines down the road along which these twenty years have taken us and shows, among other things, one symbolic sight: literature treading its own path toward extinction.

So what is to be done? I, as a writer, think of

the route taken by Japan and its future direction from the standpoint of literature. I believe that by reflecting on the cultural climate of Japan in the latter half of the 1970s and the first half of the 1980s, one can see glimpses of what course of action should be taken. What one sees during that period is the introduction, in short, accelerating cycles, of Western cultural theories adopted superficially and then dismissed. This sort of situation could only occur in a society separated by vast oceans from the countries in which they first developed, one where the introduction of those theories was done only after overcoming linguistic barriers, one dominated by a fashion-conscious intellectual journalism that transmitted those ideas to a compliant audience. With only a few exceptions, the Japanese were unable to establish a cultural theory of their own, and despite the enthusiasm they engendered, the theories imported from elsewhere essentially had nothing to do with Japan, which can be seen from the fact that they now seem as remote and foreign as they did at the very outset.

In the light of this situation, what is lacking in

terms of the cultural work being done by the Japanese today is clear enough. When Japan's effort to modernize ran into the fatal impasse of the Pacific War, the Japanese made a serious search for a set of principles to guide them in making a fresh start, and the aim of the postwar writers was to give literary expression to such principles. However, the intellectuals of the 1970s and 1980s have neither followed up on these principles nor taken a critical stance toward them. They have ignored them, turning their backs on the ambitions and actual accomplishments of that earlier generation, and severed any connection with it.

The postwar writers, after firsthand experience of the war, actively sought a direction for their country contrary to that which it had taken in the past. They envisaged a way for Japan to live as an integral part of the third world, in Asia. Prior to the defeat, Japanese intellectuals had set up the central nations of the world—Europe and America—as paradigms to follow. The postwar writers, however, looked for a different path that would lead Japan to a place in the world not at its center but on the edge of it. What the Japanese had abandoned in pursuing a center-oriented modernization, the postwar writers endeavored to revive, in part by learning domestically from Okinawa, which had a cultural tradition of its own, and internationally from South Korea, which was pursuing a typically Asian prosperity and diversity.

I would like to add that, as a writer aware of carrying on the heritage of the postwar group, I myself have always borne in mind in my own work the islands of Okinawa, a peripheral region of Japan, and the Republic of Korea, a peripheral nation in the world—and in the latter case especially the works of the modern poet Kim Chi Ha. Using "the image system of grotesque realism" as a literary weapon, and exploring the cultural characteristics of the marginal areas of my own country and Asia, I have moved along the same path, one leading toward the "relativization" of an emperor-centered culture. In that regard, the course I chose is the exact opposite of the one followed by Mishima. My novel *Contemporary Games*, which I completed at the end of the 1970s, is a work in which I aimed at creating a model of the living culture that I envisage for Japan.

Japan as a third-world nation has an ambiguous place in the world and an ambiguous role to play. Its young intellectuals have a still more ambiguous place in Japan and an equally ambiguous role to play. An examination and interpretation of these ambiguities in the light of the new cultural theories would have been a difficult task but one well worth undertaking, for I believe it would have resulted in the development of a cultural theory unique to Japan; if not, at least it would have taken us beyond the almost automatic process of "accepting" and "discharging" borrowed ideas.

Among intellectuals of the present generation, there are a few who are taking an increasing interest in the cultural idiosyncracy of Okinawan culture, and their interest corresponds to the growing self-expression of the new generation of Okinawans. Many young Japanese who participated in the protest movement for the release of the poet Kim Chi Ha still sympathize with the grass-roots campaign for democracy in South Korea. There is also an initiative concerned with keeping a close watch on Japan's economic aggression toward the Philippines and other Asian nations, and young people involved in that enterprise are now seeking an alliance with their counterparts elsewhere. The intellectuals who played a part in introducing new cultural theories could easily form a bond with these young people if they were to make an effort to interpret those theories in terms of Japan's own culture and then go on to consider how they should go about reconstructing that culture. A merger of that kind could bring about direct, concrete results in stimulating the literature of the new generation.

The subject of this symposium raises the urgent question of whether Japanese culture can find a way to save itself from the decline that its literature portends. I can think of no people as much in need of a means of self-recovery as the Japanese, neither in the third world nor the first; no other people whose culture is such a strange blend of these two worlds.

One reason I wanted to participate in it was

to learn, for the questions I have discussed loom larger for me than for younger intellectuals. But I would like to close by offering a hint to intelligent members of the new generation in the hope of giving their own search a positive direction. There was in Japan a poet and writer of children's stories, Kenji Miyazawa, who was once assigned a peripheral place in modern literary history but whose importance is now gradually being recognized. Miyazawa was born in northeastern Japan, and being an agronomist, he worked for the farmers of that remote and rugged region. He was also a believer in the Saddharma Pundarika Sutra. Under the influence of contemporary European poetry, he began to create a world of his own expression and imagination. He wrote prolifically while he worked in his chosen profession, one that he pursued until his death in 1933 at the age of thirty-seven. His audience was not limited to readers of literature as such, and posthumously he has won—and is winning—an even wider range of readers. Recently, his epic children's story, *Night Train to the Stars*, was made into an excellent animated film, increasing his popularity even more.

The question of what is genuine popular literature has been a topic of debate throughout the history of modern Japan, but now people have begun to realize that it is Miyazawa who deserves to the fullest degree the title "writer of popular literature." Sixty years ago, at the dawn of the Showa era, Miyazawa wrote a treatise called *Outline of the Essentials of Peasant Art*, which epitomizes his ideas both as an agronomist and as a writer. I would like to end by quoting its opening lines:

> We are all farmers; the work is hard and unrelenting.
>
> We seek a way to a livelier and more cheerful life, the way our ancestors lived.
>
> I want to have the sort of talk that combines the facts of modern science, the experiments of seekers of the truth, and our own intuition.
>
> No individual can be happy unless the whole world is happy.
>
> Awareness starts with the individual and gradually spreads to the

group, to society, and to the universe beyond.

Isn't this the path shown us by the saints of old?

A new age is coming when the world shall be one in its awareness and become a living entity.

Truth and strength come from being aware of the galaxy of stars within us, and living according to this knowledge.

Let us seek true happiness for the world—the search for the path is itself the path.

JAPAN, THE AMBIGUOUS, AND MYSELF

Nobel Prize Speech
Stockholm, 1994

Translated by Hisaaki Yamanouchi

During the last catastrophic World War I was a little boy and lived in a remote, wooded valley on Shikoku Island in the Japanese archipelago, thousands of miles away from here. At that time there were two books that I was really fascinated by: *The Adventures of Huckleberry Finn* and *The Wonderful Adventures of Nils*. The whole world was then engulfed by waves of horror. By reading *Huckleberry Finn* I felt I was able to justify my habit of going into the mountain forest at night and sleeping among the trees with a sense of security that I could never find indoors.

The hero of *The Wonderful Adventures of Nils* is transformed into a tiny creature who understands the language of birds and sets out on an exciting journey. I derived from the story a variety of sensuous pleasures. Firstly, living as I was in a deeply wooded area in Shikoku just as my ancestors had done long before, I found it gave me the conviction, at once innocent and unwavering, that this world and my way of life there offered me real freedom. Secondly, I felt sympathetic and identified with Nils, a naughty child who, while traveling across Sweden, collaborating with and fighting for the wild geese, grows into a different character, still innocent, yet full of confidence as well as modesty. But my greatest pleasure came from the words Nils uses when he at last comes home, and I felt purified and uplifted as if speaking with him when he says to his parents (in the French translation): " 'Maman, Papa! Je suis grand, je suis de nouveau un homme!' " ("Mother, Father! I'm a big boy, I'm a human being again!")

I was fascinated by the phrase "je suis de nouveau un homme!" in particular. As I grew up, I was to suffer continual hardships in different but related realms of life—in my family, in my relationship to Japanese society, and in my general way of living in the latter half of the twentieth century. I have survived by representing these sufferings of mine in the form of the novel. In that process I have found myself repeating, almost sighing, "je suis de nouveau un homme!" Speaking in this personal vein might seem perhaps inappropriate to this place and to this occasion. However, allow me to say that the fundamental method of my writing has always been to start from personal matters and then to link them with society, the state, and the world in general. I hope you will forgive me for talking about these personal things a little longer.

Half a century ago, while living in the depths of that forest, I read *The Wonderful Adventures of Nils* and felt within it two prophecies. One was that I might one day be able to understand the language of birds. The other was that I might one day fly off with my beloved wild geese—preferably to Scandinavia.

After I got married, the first child born to us was mentally handicapped. We named him Hikari, meaning "light" in Japanese. As a baby he responded only to the chirping of wild birds and never to human voices. One summer when he was six years old we were staying at our country cottage. He heard a pair of water rails calling from the lake beyond a grove, and with the voice of a commentator on a recording of birdsong he said:

"Those are water rails." These were the first words my son had ever uttered. It was from then on that my wife and I began communicating verbally with him.

Hikari now works at a vocational training center for the handicapped, an institution based on ideas learned from Sweden. In the meantime he has been composing works of music. Birds were the things that occasioned and mediated his composition of human music. On my behalf Hikari has thus fulfilled the prophecy that I might one day understand the language of birds. I must also say that my life would have been impossible but for my wife with her abundant female strength and wisdom. She has been the very incarnation of Akka, the leader of Nils's wild geese. Together we have flown to Stockholm, and so the second of the prophecies has also, to my great delight, now been realized.

Yasunari Kawabata, the first Japanese writer to stand on this platform as a Nobel laureate for literature, delivered a lecture entitled "Japan, the Beautiful, and Myself." It was at once very beautiful and very vague. I use the word "vague" as an equivalent of the Japanese *aimaina*, itself a word open to several interpretations. The kind of vagueness that Kawabata deliberately adopted is implied even in the title of his lecture, with the use of the Japanese particle *no* (literally "of") linking "Myself" and "Beautiful Japan." One way of reading it is "myself as a part of beautiful Japan," the *no* indicating the relationship of the noun following it to the noun preceding it as one of possession or attachment. It can also be understood as "beautiful Japan and myself," the particle in this case linking the two nouns in apposition, which is how they appear in the English title of Kawabata's lecture as translated by Professor Edward Seidensticker, one of the most eminent American specialists in Japanese literature. His expert translation—"Japan, the beautiful, *and* myself"—is that of a *traduttore* (translator) and in no way a *traditore* (traitor).

Under that title Kawabata talked about a unique kind of mysticism which is found not only in Japanese thought but also more widely in Oriental philosophy. By "unique" I mean here a tendency toward Zen Buddhism. Even as a twentieth-century writer Kawabata identified his own mentality with that affirmed in poems written by medieval Zen monks. Most of these poems are concerned with the linguistic impossibility of telling the truth. Words, according to such poems, are confined within closed shells, and the reader cannot expect them ever to emerge, to get through to us. Instead, to understand or respond to Zen poems one must abandon oneself and willingly enter into the closed shells of those words.

Why did Kawabata boldly decide to read those very esoteric poems in Japanese before the audience in Stockholm? I look back almost with nostalgia on the straightforward courage he attained toward the end of his distinguished career which enabled him to make such a confession of his faith. Kawabata had been an artistic pilgrim for decades during which he produced a series of masterpieces. After those years of pilgrimage, it was only by talking of his fascination with poetry that baffled any attempt fully to understand it that he was able to talk about "Japan, the Beautiful, and Myself"; in other words, about the world he lived in and the literature he created.

It is noteworthy, too, that Kawabata concluded his lecture as follows:

> My works have been described as
> works of emptiness, but it is not to
> be taken for the nihilism of the West.
> The spiritual foundation would seem
> to be quite different. Dogen entitled
> his poem about the seasons "Innate
> Reality," and even as he sang of the
> beauty of the seasons he was deeply
> immersed in Zen.
>
> (Translation by Edward Seidensticker)

Here also I detect a brave and straightforward self-assertion. Not only did Kawabata identify himself as belonging essentially to the tradition of Zen philosophy and aesthetic sensibility pervading the classical literature of the Orient, but he went out of his way to differentiate emptiness as an attribute of his works from the nihilism of the West. By doing so he was wholeheartedly addressing the coming generations of mankind in whom Alfred Nobel placed his hope and faith.

To tell the truth, however, instead of my compatriot who stood here twenty-six years ago, I feel more spiritual affinity with the Irish poet William Butler Yeats, who was awarded a Nobel Prize for Literature seventy-one years ago when he was about the same age as me. Of course I make no claim to being in the same rank as that poetic genius; I am merely a humble follower living in a country far removed from his. But as William Blake, whose work Yeats reevaluated and restored to the high place it holds in this century, once wrote: "Across Europe & Asia to China & Japan like lightenings."

During the last few years I have been engaged in writing a trilogy which I wish to be the culmination of my literary activities. So far the first two parts have been published, and I have recently finished writing the third and final part. It is entitled in Japanese *A Flaming Green Tree*. I am indebted for this title to a stanza from one of Yeats's important poems, "Vacillation":

> A tree there is that from its topmost bough
> Is half all glittering flame and half all green

Abounding foliage moistened with the dew....
    ("Vacillation," 11–13)

My trilogy, in fact, is permeated by the influence of Yeats's work as a whole.

On the occasion of his winning the Nobel Prize the Irish Senate proposed a motion to congratulate him, which contained the following sentences:

> ... the recognition which the nation has gained, as a prominent contributor to the world's culture, through his success ... a race that hitherto had not been accepted into the comity of nations....

> Our civilisation will be assessed on the name of Senator Yeats. Coming at a time when there was a regular wave of destruction [and] hatred of beauty ... it is a very happy and welcome thing.... [T]here will always be the danger that there may be a stampeding of people who are sufficiently

removed from insanity in enthusiasm
for destruction.

(The Nobel Prize: Congratulations to
Senator Yeats)

Yeats is the writer in whose wake I would like
to follow. I would like to do so for the sake of
another nation that has now been "accepted into
the comity of nations" not on account of literature
or philosophy but for its technology in electronic
engineering and its manufacture of motorcars.
Also I would like to do so as a citizen of a nation
that in the recent past was stampeded into "insanity in enthusiasm for destruction" both on its own
soil and on that of neighboring nations.

As someone living in present-day Japan and
sharing bitter memories of the past, I cannot join
Kawabata in saying "Japan, the Beautiful, and
Myself." A moment ago I referred to the "vagueness" of the title and content of his lecture. In the
rest of my own lecture I would like to use the
word "ambiguous," in accordance with the dis-
tinction made by the eminent British poet Kath-
leen Raine, who once said of Blake that he was not

so much vague as ambiguous. It is only in terms of "Japan, the Ambiguous, and Myself" that I can talk about myself.

After a hundred and twenty years of modernization since the opening up of the country, contemporary Japan is split between two opposite poles of ambiguity. This ambiguity, which is so powerful and penetrating that it divides both the state and its people, and affects me as a writer like a deep-felt scar, is evident in various ways. The modernization of Japan was oriented toward learning from and imitating the West, yet the country is situated in Asia and has firmly maintained its traditional culture. The ambiguous orientation of Japan drove the country into the position of an invader in Asia, and resulted in its isolation from other Asian nations not only politically but also socially and culturally. And even in the West, to which its culture was supposedly quite open, it has long remained inscrutable or only partially understood.

In the history of modern Japanese literature, the writers most sincere in their awareness of a mission were the "postwar school" of writers who

came onto the literary scene deeply wounded
by the catastrophe of war yet full of hope for a
rebirth. They tried with great pain to make up for
the atrocities committed by Japanese military
forces in Asia, as well as to bridge the profound
gaps that existed not only between the developed
nations of the West and Japan but also between
African and Latin American countries and Japan.
Only by doing so did they think that they could
seek with some humility reconciliation with the
rest of the world. It has always been my aspiration
to cling to the very end of the line of that literary
tradition inherited from those writers.

The present nation of Japan and its people
cannot but be ambivalent. The Second World War
came right in the middle of the process of modernization, a war that was brought about by the very
aberration of that process itself. Defeat in this
conflict fifty years ago created an opportunity for
Japan, as the aggressor, to attempt a rebirth out of
the great misery and suffering that the "postwar
school" of writers depicted in their work. The
moral props for a nation aspiring to this goal
were the idea of democracy and the determination

never to wage a war again—a resolve adopted not by innocent people but people stained by their own history of territorial invasion. Those moral props mattered also in regard to the victims of the nuclear weapons that were used for the first time in Hiroshima and Nagasaki, and for the survivors and their offspring affected by radioactivity (including tens of thousands of those whose mother tongue is Korean).

In recent years there have been criticisms leveled against Japan suggesting that it should offer more military support to the United Nations forces and thereby play a more active role in the keeping and restoration of peace in various parts of the world. Our hearts sink whenever we hear these comments. After the Second World War it was a categorical imperative for Japan to renounce war forever as a central article of the new constitution. The Japanese chose, after their painful experiences, the principle of permanent peace as the moral basis for their rebirth.

I believe that this principle can best be understood in the West, with its long tradition of tolerance for conscientious objection to military service.

In Japan itself there have all along been attempts by some people to remove the article about renunciation of war from the constitution, and for this purpose they have taken every opportunity to make use of pressure from abroad. But to remove the principle of permanent peace would be an act of betrayal toward the people of Asia and the victims of the bombs dropped on Hiroshima and Nagasaki. It is not difficult for me as a writer to imagine the outcome.

The prewar Japanese constitution, which posited an absolute power transcending the principle of democracy, was sustained by a degree of support from the general public. Even though our new constitution is already half a century old, there is still a popular feeling of support for the old one, which lives on in some quarters as something more substantial than mere nostalgia. If Japan were to institutionalize a principle other than the one to which we have adhered for the last fifty years, the determination we made in the postwar ruins of our collapsed effort at modernization—that determination of ours to establish the concept of universal humanity—would come to nothing. Speaking as an ordinary individual, this is the specter that rises before me.

What I call Japan's "ambiguity" in this lecture is a kind of chronic disease that has been prevalent throughout the modern age. Japan's economic prosperity is not free from it either, accompanied as it is by all kinds of potential dangers in terms of the structure of the world economy and environmental conservation. The "ambiguity" in this respect seems to be accelerating. It may be more obvious to the critical eyes of the world at large than to us in our own country. At the nadir of postwar poverty we found a resilience to endure it, never losing our hope of recovery. It may sound curious to say so, but we seem to have no less resilience in enduring our anxiety about the future of the present tremendous prosperity. And a new situation now seems to be arising in which Japan's wealth assumes a growing share of the potential power of both production and consumption in Asia as a whole.

I am a writer who wishes to create serious works of literature distinct from those novels which are mere reflections of the vast consumer culture of Tokyo and the subcultures of the world at large. My profession—my "habit of being" (in Flannery O'Connor's words)—is that of the novelist who, as Auden described him, must:

> …, among the Just
> Be just, among the Filthy filthy too,
> And in his own weak person, if he can,
> Must suffer dully all the wrongs of Man.
> ("The Novelist," 12–14)

What, as a writer, do I see as the sort of character we Japanese should seek to have? Among the words that George Orwell often used to describe the traits he admired in people was "decent," along with "humane" and "sane." This deceptively simple term stands in stark contrast to the "ambiguous" of my own characterization, a contrast matched by the wide discrepancy between how the Japanese actually appear to others and how they would like to appear to them.

Orwell, I hope, would not have objected to my using the word "decent" as a synonym of the French *humaniste*, because both terms have in common the qualities of tolerance and humanity.

In the past, Japan too had some pioneers who tried hard to build up the "decent" or "humanistic" side of ourselves. One such person was the late Professor Kazuo Watanabe, a scholar of French Renaissance literature and thought. Surrounded by the insane patriotic ardor of Japan on the eve and in the throes of the Second World War, Watanabe had a lonely dream of grafting the humanistic view of man onto the traditional Japanese sense of beauty and sensitivity to nature, which fortunately had not been entirely eradicated. (I hasten to add that Watanabe's conception of beauty and nature was different from that of Kawabata as expressed in his "Japan, the Beautiful, and Myself.") The way Japan had tried to construct a modern state modeled on the West was a disaster. In ways different from yet partly corresponding to that process, Japanese intellectuals tried to bridge the gap between the West and their own country at its deepest level. It must have been an arduous task but also one that sometimes brimmed with satisfaction.

Watanabe's study of François Rabelais was one of the most distinguished scholarly achievements of the Japanese intellectual world. When, as a student in prewar Paris, he told his academic supervisor about his ambition to translate Rabelais into Japanese, the eminent, elderly French scholar answered the young man with the phrase: "L'entreprise inouïe de la traduction de l'intraduisible Rabelais" (the unprecedented enterprise of translating into Japanese untranslatable Rabelais). Another French scholar answered with blunt astonishment: "Belle entreprise Pantagruélique" (an admirably Pantagruelian undertaking). In spite of all this, not only did Watanabe accomplish his ambitious project in circumstances of great poverty during the war and the American occupation, but he also did his best to transplant into the confused and disoriented Japan of that time the life and thought of those French humanists who were the forerunners, contemporaries, and followers of Rabelais.

In both my life and writing I have been a pupil of Professor Watanabe's. I was influenced by him in two crucial ways. One was in my method of writing novels. I learned concretely from his translation of Rabelais what Mikhail Bakhtin formulated as "the image system of grotesque realism or the culture of popular laughter": the importance of material and physical principles; the correspondence between the cosmic, social, and physical elements; the overlapping of death and a passion for rebirth; and the laughter that subverts established hierarchical relationships.

The image system made it possible to seek literary methods of attaining the universal for someone like me, born and brought up in a peripheral, marginal, off-center region of a peripheral, marginal, off-center country. Coming from such a background, I do not represent Asia as a new economic power but Asia marked by everlasting poverty and a tumultuous fertility. By sharing old, familiar, yet living metaphors I align myself with writers like Kim Chi Ha of Korea, or Chon I and Mu Jen, both of China. For me the brotherhood of world literature consists of such relationships in positive, concrete terms. I once took part in a hunger strike for the political freedom of a gifted Korean poet. I am now deeply worried about the fate of those talented Chinese novelists who have been deprived of their freedom since the Tiananmen Square incident.

Another way in which Professor Watanabe has influenced me is in his idea of humanism. I take it to be the quintessence of Europe as a living entity. It is an idea that is also explicit in Milan Kundera's definition of the novel. Based on his accurate reading of historical sources, Watanabe wrote critical biographies, with Rabelais at their center, of people from Erasmus to Sébastien Castellion, and of women connected with Henri IV from Queen Marguerite to Gabrielle d'Estrées. By doing so he hoped to teach the Japanese about humanism, about the importance of tolerance, about man's vulnerability to his preconceptions and to the machinery of his own making. His sincerity led him to quote the remark by the Danish philologist Kristoffer Nyrop: "Those who do not protest against war are accomplices of war." In his attempt to transplant into Japan humanism as the very basis of Western thought Watanabe was bravely venturing on both "l'entreprise inouïe" and the "belle entreprise Pantagruélique."

As someone influenced by his thought, I wish my work as a novelist to help both those who express themselves in words and their readers to overcome their own sufferings and the sufferings of their time, and to cure their souls of their wounds. I have said that I am split between the opposite poles of an ambiguity characteristic of the Japanese. The pain this involves I have tried to remove by means of literature. I can only hope and pray that my fellow Japanese will in time recover from it too.

If you will allow me to mention him again, my son Hikari was awakened by the voices of birds to the music of Bach and Mozart, eventually composing his own works. The little pieces that he first produced had a radiant freshness and delight in them; they seemed like dew glittering on leaves of grass. The word "innocence" is composed of *in* and *nocere*, or "not to hurt." Hikari's music was in this sense a natural effusion of the composer's own innocence.

As Hikari went on to produce more works, I began to hear in his music also "the voice of a crying and dark soul." Handicapped though he was, his hard-won "habit of being"—composing—acquired a growing maturity of technique and a deepening of conception. That in turn enabled him to discover in the depth of his heart a mass of dark sorrow which until then he had been unable to express.

"The voice of a crying and dark soul" is beautiful, and the act of setting it to music cures him of this sorrow, becoming an act of recovery. His music, moreover, has been widely accepted as one that cures and restores other listeners as well. In this I find grounds for believing in the wondrous healing power of art.

There is no firm proof of this belief of mine, but "weak person" though I am, with the aid of this unverifiable belief, I would like to "suffer dully all the wrongs" accumulated throughout this century as a result of the uncontrolled development of inhuman technology. As one with a peripheral, marginal, off-center existence in the world, I would like to continue to seek—with what I hope is a modest, decent, humanistic contribution of my own—ways to be of some use in the cure and reconciliation of mankind.